#35
Sunland-Tujunga Branch Library
7771 Foothill Boulevard
Tujunga, CA 91042

 **W9-BRD-009**

THIRTY-FIVE
JUN 07 2011

x
629.3
T559

2006 32355

HOVERCRAFT

Sarah Tieck

Amazing Vehicles

Big Buddy BOOKS
Amazing Vehicles

ABDO
Publishing Company

VISIT US AT
www.abdopublishing.com

Published by ABDO Publishing Company, 8000 West 78th Street, Edina, Minnesota 55439.

Copyright © 2011 by Abdo Consulting Group, Inc. International copyrights reserved in all countries. No part of this book may be reproduced in any form without written permission from the publisher. Big Buddy Books™ is a trademark and logo of ABDO Publishing Company.

Printed in the United States of America, North Mankato, Minnesota.
102010
012011

 PRINTED ON RECYCLED PAPER

Coordinating Series Editor: Rochelle Baltzer
Contributing Editors: Megan M. Gunderson, BreAnn Rumsch, Marcia Zappa
Graphic Design: Deb Coldiron, Maria Hosley, Marcia Zappa
Cover Photograph: *Getty Images*: Purestock.
Interior Photographs/Illustrations: *AP Photo*: AP Photo (p. 29), Press Association via AP Images (p. 25), Xinhua, Qiu Qilong (p. 23), Obed Zilwa (p. 23); *Fotosearch*: Purestock (p. 15); *Getty Images*: Getty Images (pp. 19, 27, 30), JENS KOEHLER/AFP (p. 7), National Geographic (p. 7), Purestock (pp. 10, 12, 16, 18, 22, 26, 28), Travel Ink (p. 9); *iStockphoto*: ©iStockphoto.com/nicksliced (p. 29); ©iStockphoto.com/vandervelden (p. 13); *Thinkstock*: iStockphoto (pp. 5, 11, 17); *U.S. Marine Corps*: Lance Cpl. Joshua A. Rucker (pp. 7, 21); *U.S. Navy*: Mass Communication Specialist 2nd Class Julio Rivera (p. 21), Mass Communication Specialist 2nd Class Jason R. Zalasky (p. 21).

Library of Congress Cataloging-in-Publication Data

Tieck, Sarah, 1976-
  Hovercraft / Sarah Tieck.
    p. cm. -- (Amazing vehicles)
  ISBN 978-1-61714-698-5
  1. Ground-effect machines--Juvenile literature. 2. Hydrofoil boats--Juvenile literature. I. Title.
  VM363.T54 2011
  629.3--dc22
                              2010028578

CONTENTS

GET MOVING

Imagine riding on a hovercraft. The engines roar and wet air brushes your cheeks. You are flying above the water's surface!

Have you ever looked closely at a hovercraft? Many parts work together to make it move. A hovercraft is an amazing vehicle!

A hovercraft is also called an air-cushion vehicle (ACV).

WHAT IS A HOVERCRAFT?

A hovercraft can move over land and water. Instead of moving on the surface, it hovers on air just above it.

Hovercraft come in many shapes and sizes. Their features depend on their use. Most are made to be safe, strong, and easy to use.

Hovercraft can travel over ice, snow, mud, sand, and marshes!

A CLOSER LOOK

Hovercraft are made of sturdy, lightweight parts. Because a hovercraft can move over water, some features are like a boat's. Other hovercraft parts are like an airplane's. **Propellers** help a hovercraft move.

HOVERTRAVEL

RYDE ORTSMOUTH

6

5

4

1

HOVERCRAFT

8

1. The **skirt** traps air underneath the hovercraft. This creates a cushion.

2. A hovercraft's **propellers** look like large fans. They help the hovercraft move forward.

3. **Rudders** steer a hovercraft. Airplanes and boats also have rudders.

4. People and objects may fit on a hovercraft's **deck**.

5. A large hovercraft has a bent pipe on each side called a **bow thruster**. It lets out air from the lift fans, which are below the vehicle.

6. The **cockpit** has a control station. This is where the pilot sits.

API · 88/100

GH · 2114

HOW DOES IT LIFT?

A hovercraft has at least one powerful engine. Some have more than one engine. A hovercraft's engine powers one or more lift fans.

Lift fans pull in air and spin. As they spin, they push the air into the hovercraft's skirt. The skirt hangs under the hovercraft. As it fills with air, it swells like a balloon.

Water or sand may spray up in a cloud around a hovercraft. Airflow from the hovercraft's lift fans causes this to happen.

FAST FACT: Sometimes hovercraft pilots talk about "getting over the hump." This is the amount of time it takes to get off the water and fly.

The skirt holds the trapped air under the hovercraft. This high-**pressure** air blows onto the ground or water surface. It is so powerful that it lifts the hovercraft and keeps it in the air.

Some hovercraft have finger skirts. These skirts have narrow sections that press together when filled with air.

HOW DOES IT MOVE?

A force called thrust moves a hovercraft forward. This force comes from a hovercraft's large **propellers**. They have blades shaped like an airplane's wing.

The hovercraft's engine powers the propellers. As the blades spin, they pull in air from the front. When the air blows out the back, it pushes the hovercraft forward.

14

Propellers are protected inside large screens. This keeps out flying objects.

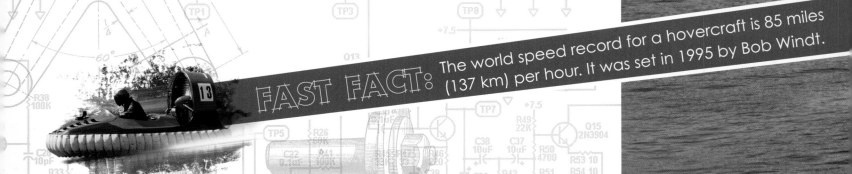

To operate a hovercraft, the pilot uses controls. These start the engine and change the hovercraft's speed. They also allow the pilot to turn the vehicle.

Small hovercraft have a few simple controls. Large hovercraft have rooms called cockpits. A cockpit has pedals, buttons, and radios to operate the hovercraft.

A hovercraft's cockpit can be large enough for more than one pilot.

FAST FACT: Small hovercraft may have a safety cord that hooks on the driver's wrist. If the driver falls off, the cord pulls out. This shuts down the engine.

THE PILOT'S SEAT

Hovercraft are fun and exciting! But, they can also be hard to control. It takes practice and skill to operate them safely.

There are few rules for how hovercraft are made and used. When they are over water, hovercraft are considered boats. So, pilots must know their state's boating laws and rules. On land, they may not be used on public roads.

Hovercraft pilots must be safe drivers. Vehicle crashes can cause injuries or damage.

PROTECT AND SERVE

The military uses hovercraft. Large hovercraft, such as the Landing Craft Air Cushion (LCAC), carry troops and supplies. They move tanks and weapons between ships and land. This keeps soldiers and objects safe and dry.

Hovercraft help with search-and-rescue efforts, too. They allow soldiers to travel through places that are hard to reach.

An LCAC has several crew members. They direct people on board and secure the load.

An LCAC sets off from a large ship. It can fly onto a beach (*left*) or land on another ship (*below*).

21

FAST FACT: Hovercraft are loud! So, drivers may wear earplugs to protect their hearing.

PRACTICAL MAGIC

Businesses such as hotels and golf courses use hovercraft. Hovercraft move guests from place to place.

Scientists and park rangers also use hovercraft. They drive them in natural areas that other vehicles cannot reach. Since hovercraft don't have wheels, they are less harmful to nature.

Hovercraft help people travel through icy areas where boats or cars cannot go.

Some grounds crews use hovercraft to dry wet sports fields!

FUN, FUN, FUN!

Some people own hovercraft for fun and **recreation**. They may use hovercraft like boats for fishing or cruising. Some hovercraft have space to seat many people. Others are made for one person.

24

It is fun to ride on hovercraft in nice weather. But, they can also be used in snow or other types of weather!

FAST FACT: The world's first hovercraft race was held in 1964 in Canberra, Australia.

PLAYING CATCH-UP

Around the world, people use hovercraft for sports. Hovercraft races are popular. Pilots race on land or water tracks. They go very fast and do sharp turns!

Most hovercraft don't have brakes. To stop, a racer may spin the craft and then blast the engines. This makes for a powerful finish to the race!

FAST FACT: Cockerell used a blower and two small cans to test his hovercraft ideas.

PAST TO PRESENT

Starting in the 1870s, people had the idea to make air-cushion vehicles. In 1956, Sir Christopher Cockerell made the first operating hovercraft. So, he is considered the father of the hovercraft.

Today, many people consider the hovercraft a successful invention. People use these vehicles to race, rescue, **protect**, and play. Hovercraft are amazing vehicles!

Cockerell created the SR.N1 hovercraft (*left*). In 1959, it made its first flight. Today's hovercraft have improved features.

BLAST FROM THE PAST

Hovercraft were first used by the U.S. military during the **Vietnam War**. Vietnam is a country with many watery areas. The U.S. Navy used the Patrol Air Cushion Vehicle (PACV) along rivers and coastlines. Smaller hovercraft allowed soldiers to move through **marshes**.

IMPORTANT WORDS

marsh an area of low, wet land.

pressure (PREH-shuhr) the pushing of a force against an opposing force.

propeller an object consisting of blades mounted on a bar. An engine turns the bar, which makes the blades spin. This motion moves vehicles such as boats, airplanes, or helicopters.

protect (pruh-TEHKT) to guard against harm or danger.

recreation (reh-kree-AY-shuhn) an activity done in free time for fun or enjoyment.

Vietnam War a war that took place between South Vietnam and North Vietnam from 1957 to 1975. The United States was involved in this war for many years.

WEB SITES

To learn more about hovercraft, visit ABDO Publishing Company online. Web sites about hovercraft are featured on our Book Links page. These links are routinely monitored and updated to provide the most current information available.

www.abdopublishing.com

INDEX